About Skill Builders Algebra I

by Tracy Dankberg

Welcome to RBP Books' Skill Builders series. Like our Summer Bridge Activities collection, the Skill Builders series is designed to make learning both fun and rewarding.

Skill Builders Algebra provides students with focused practice to help them reinforce and develop math skills. Each Skill Builders volume is grade-level appropriate, with clear examples and instructions to guide the lesson. In accordance with NCTM standards, the algebra exercises in this book cover a variety of math skills, including exponents, evaluating and writing algebraic expressions, equations, integers and rational numbers, working with inequalities, monomials and polynomials, factoring, quadratic equations, graphing, and linear equations.

A critical thinking section includes problem-solving exercises to help develop higher-order thinking skills.

Learning is more effective when approached with an element of fun and enthusiasm—just as most children approach life. That's why the Skill Builders combine entertaining and academically sound exercises and fun themes to make reviewing basic skills fun and effective, for both you and your budding scholars.

Table of Contents

Exponential Notation

Evaluate each expression.

Example:

$(2x)^3$ if $x = 2$

$(2 \cdot 2)^3 = 4^3 = \mathbf{64}$

1. y^3 if $y = 5$

2. m^1 if $m = 21$

3. $3n^5$ if $n = 2$

4. $(3n)^5$ if $n = 2$

5. $x^3 - 5$ if $x = 2$

6. $3y^4 + 5$ if $y = 3$

7. x^2y if $x = 4, y = 5$

8. $c^2 + c$ if $c = 5$

9. $5xy^2$ if $x = 5, y = 2$

10. $4m^0$ if $m = 5$

Evaluating Algebraic Expressions

Evaluate each expression.

Example:

$(10 - x)^2$ if $x = 2$

$(10 - 2)^2 = 8^2 = \textbf{64}$

1. $(3y)^2 - 5$ if $y = 3$

2. $5(x + 10)$ if $x = 5$

3. $m + 6m^2$ if $m = 4$

4. $(c - 5)^3$ if $c = 6$

5. $(n + 6)(n - 2)$ if $n = 12$

6. $\dfrac{c + 10}{2c}$ if $c = 10$

7. $\dfrac{y^2 + 2}{3y}$ if $y = 4$

8. $x^0 + 2x^1$ if $x = 20$

9. $\dfrac{(5x) + 5}{5x}$ if $x = 1$

10. $\dfrac{3a^2 + a}{a}$ if $a = 4$

Writing Algebraic Expressions

Write each phrase as an algebraic expression.

Example:

4 less than a number

n – 4

1. 5 more than x

2. c less than 5

3. p added to 10

4. the product of 3 and h

5. half of y

6. three times a number

7. a number increased by three times x

8. a number y increased by itself

9. three less than twice x

10. 2 more than the product of 6 and y

11. the quotient of a number divided by 10

12. the perimeter of a square with sides length s

©RBP Books   Algebra I Grades 5–8—RBP0105

Solving Equations Using Addition and Subtraction

Solve each equation.

Example:

$$y + 57 = 119$$
$$y = 119 - 57$$
$$\mathbf{y = 62}$$

1. $x + 2.6 = 9.8$

2. $m - 37 = 312$

3. $a - 12 = 101$

4. $x + 89 = 376$

5. $c + 2.04 = 3.68$

6. $y - 1{,}064 = 3{,}882$

7. $a + \dfrac{2}{7} = \dfrac{6}{7}$

8. $p - \dfrac{4}{15} = \dfrac{3}{5}$

9. $6.44 = x + 1.78$

10. $23 = y - 261$

www.summerbridgeactivities.com

©RBP Books

Solving Equations Using Multiplication and Division

Solve each equation.

Example:

$$9m = 108$$
$$m = \frac{108}{9}$$
$$\mathbf{m = 12}$$

1. $26m = 182$

2. $102 = 17c$

3. $\dfrac{x}{0.11} = 6$

4. $\dfrac{m}{6} = 62$

5. $3p = 183$

6. $5.44 = 0.34a$

7. $59 = \dfrac{x}{4}$

8. $\dfrac{r}{0.2} = 4.8$

9. $23y = 115$

10. $9m = 3.6$

Solve by writing an equation.

1. The product of a number and 7 is 63.

2. An independent contractor charges $60 per hour. How many hours did the contractor work to make $42,720?

3. Mary paid $5.00 for a dozen bagels. About how much does one bagel cost?

4. Nancy scored a 75 on her second math test. That was 12 points less than her score on the first math test. What was her score on the first test?

5. There are 324 golf balls on the driving range. If half of them are white, how many white golf balls are there?

6. Michael has saved $56.25. He wants to buy a pair of $70 shoes. How much more money does he need to save?

Integers

Part I: Evaluate.

**:** The absolute value of a number is its distance from zero on a number line.

$|{-12}| = \mathbf{12}$ because -12 is 12 places from zero.

1. $|{-35}|$

2. $|6.8|$

3. $|{-4}| + |{-5}|$

4. $|13| + |{-13}|$

5. $|{-8}| \cdot |{-2}|$

6. $|{-5}| \cdot |{-7}| \cdot |0|$

Part II: Order from least to greatest.

**:**

$15, -21, -15 = \mathbf{-21, -15, 15}$

7. $14, -13, 6, -16$

8. $-33, 5, 0, -18$

9. $-34, -36, -28, -32, -4$

10. $14, -24, -14, -6, 6$

Part I: Use <, >, or = to make each statement true.

Example:

2.42 $\bigcirc$< 2.52

because 42 hundredths is less than 52 hundredths

1. -3.23 $\bigcirc$ -5.2

2. 224 $\bigcirc$ -400

3. -0.505 $\bigcirc$ -0.550

4. $\frac{-4}{9}$ $\bigcirc$ $\frac{2}{5}$

5. -16.25 $\bigcirc$ -17

6. $\frac{5}{3}$ $\bigcirc$ $\frac{7}{5}$

Part II: Order from least to greatest.

7. $\frac{7}{5}$, $\frac{-1}{8}$, $\frac{-4}{5}$

8. $\frac{-2}{3}$, $\frac{1}{2}$, $\frac{-3}{4}$, $\frac{1}{6}$

9. $\frac{5}{8}$, $\frac{1}{8}$, $\frac{-8}{8}$, $\frac{-5}{8}$

10. $\frac{4}{2}$, $\frac{4}{5}$, $\frac{4}{9}$, $\frac{4}{8}$

Find each sum.

Example:

Two Negatives	One Negative, One Positive
$^-14 + (^-8) = ^-\mathbf{22}$	$^-4 + 22 = \mathbf{18}$
$|^-14| + |^-8| =$	$|22| - |^-4| =$
$14 + 8 = 22$	$22 - 4 = 18$
The sign is negative because both addends are negative.	The sign is positive because 22 is the greater absolute value.

1. $23 + (^-7) =$

2. $^-10 + (^-10) =$

3. $^-3.24 + 17.1 =$

4. $0.08 + (^-0.15) =$

5. $\dfrac{^-2}{5} + \dfrac{3}{5} =$

6. $\dfrac{^-3}{7} + (\dfrac{^-4}{7}) =$

7. $\dfrac{1}{18} + (\dfrac{^-5}{9}) =$

8. $\dfrac{^-1}{8} + (\dfrac{^-1}{3}) =$

9. $^-16 + 28 + (^-5) =$

10. $455 + (^-123) + (^-615) =$

Find each difference.

Example:

When subtracting rational numbers, add the opposite.

$$^-6.5 - (^-8.1) = \mathbf{1.6}$$
$$^-6.5 + 8.1 = \mathbf{1.6}$$

1. $4 - 10 =$

2. $^-11 - (^-11) =$

3. $11 - (^-11) =$

4. $^-5 - (^-12) =$

5. $0 - (^-300) =$

6. $^-3.8 - 1.1 =$

7. $7 - (^-6.3) =$

8. $4 - 5.53 =$

9. $\frac{^-3}{8} - (\frac{^-1}{4}) =$

10. $\frac{1}{13} - \frac{1}{12} =$

Find each product.

Example:

$$-8(-4.2) = \mathbf{33.6} \qquad\qquad -3 \cdot 16 = \mathbf{^-48}$$
$$9 \cdot 5 = \mathbf{45} \qquad\qquad\qquad 4(-5) = \mathbf{^-20}$$

1. $-6(-7) =$

2. $12(-10) =$

3. $-25(48) =$

4. $-87(-2.1) =$

5. $\dfrac{-1}{5}\left(\dfrac{2}{9}\right) =$

6. $\dfrac{5}{7}\left(\dfrac{-7}{2}\right) =$

7. $-12(-26)(0) =$

8. $-3(-4)(-5) =$

9. $-3(-4)(-5)(-6) =$

10. $0.03(-3)(2.3) =$

Find each quotient.

$$-32 \div 4 = -8$$
$$32 \div (-4) = -8$$
$$-32 \div (-4) = 8$$

$$\frac{-3}{5} \div \frac{9}{7} =$$

$$\frac{-3^1}{5} \cdot \frac{7}{9_3} = \frac{-7}{15}$$

1. $48 \div (-12)$

2. $-63 \div 7$

3. $\frac{72}{-9}$

4. $\frac{-108}{12}$

5. $\frac{0}{-4}$

6. $-200 \div (0)$

7. $\frac{5}{8} \div \frac{6}{5}$

8. $\frac{-3}{5} \div (\frac{-5}{3})$

9. $\frac{-3}{4} \div \frac{2}{3}$

10. $1\frac{1}{5} \div (\frac{-5}{12})$

Using the Distributive Property

Simplify.

Example:

$8(y - 4) = 8y - 8(4)$
$= 8y - 32$

1. $7(x - 7)$

2. $^-5(y - 4)$

3. $3(x - 2y)$

4. $^-4(x - 2y + 3)$

5. $6(3x - 4y + 8z)$

6. $2.1(^-1.2x + 2.3y - 1.1)$

7. $^-8(3x + 2y - 6)$

8. $3(4a - 5b + 7)$

9. $\frac{2}{3}(6x - 9y)$

10. $\frac{-5}{6}(x - \frac{1}{2}y + 12)$

Algebra I Grades 5–8—RBP0105

Collect the like terms.

Example:

$$4x + 5y - 6x - 2y = 4x - 6x + 5y - 2y$$
$$= (4 - 6)x + (5 - 2)y$$
$$= {}^-2x + 3y$$

1. $5y - y$

2. $x - 4x$

3. $3a + 2a$

4. $m - 0.5m$

5. $11x + 3y - 5x$

6. $6y + 3z - 3y$

7. $13a - 13b - 13c + 15a$

8. $6p + 2p - 18$

9. $\frac{2}{5}y + \frac{3}{5}x + \frac{1}{5}y - \frac{2}{5}x$

10. $17a + 18b - 20b + a$

Simplifying Algebraic Expressions

Simplify each algebraic expression.

Example:

$$4a - 3 - (2a - 5) = 4a - 3 - 2a + 5$$
$$= 4a - 2a - 3 + 5$$
$$= \mathbf{2a + 2}$$

1. $6y - (3y + 10)$

2. $2x - (2x + 5)$

3. $4b - (6b - 8)$

4. $12m - (6m - 5)$

5. $2y + 8y - (6y + 12)$

6. $5x + 6x - (3x + 5)$

7. $3y - 4x - 2(4x - 5y)$

8. $6a - 3b + 2(b + 5a)$

9. $^-(5a - 3x) - (3x - 5a)$

10. $(^-6x + y) - (3y - 5x)$

© RBP Books   Algebra I Grades 5–8—RBP0105

Solving Two-Step Equations

Solve each equation.

Example:

$$^-3x + 5 = 26$$
$$^-3x = 26 - 5$$
$$\frac{^-3x}{^-3} = \frac{21}{^-3}$$
$$x = {}^-7$$

1. $7y + 9 = 72$

2. $4x - 6 = 38$

3. $7a + 2 = {}^-47$

4. $5m + 4 = {}^-51$

5. $^-3x + 9 = {}^-24$

6. $^-6y - 18 = {}^-84$

7. $^-4x + 83 = {}^-1$

8. $4 - 8m = 20$

9. $9y - 8 = {}^-80$

10. $^-18 - 3y = {}^-57$

Solving Equations with Variables on Both Sides

Solve each equation.

Example:

$$3y - 3 = {}^-2y + 2$$
$$3y + 2y - 3 = 2$$
$$5y = 2 + 3$$
$$5y = 5$$
$$y = 1$$

1. $3m = 4m - 14$

2. $7x = 2x + 5$

3. $3x - 5 = 5 - 2x$

4. $2a - 1 = 4 + 5a$

5. $3b - 7b + 35 = 15 - 2b$

6. $20 - 3m = 2m - 8m + 50$

7. $6y - (3y + 9) = 17$

8. $3x - 10 = 5(x - 4)$

9. $3(y - 2) = 5(y + 2)$

10. $6(6n - 1) = 7(5n - 2)$

Solving Equations Involving Absolute Value

Solve each equation.

$$|x| + 3 = 14 \qquad\qquad |x + 6| = 21$$
$$|x| = 14 - 3 \qquad\qquad x + 6 = 21 \text{ or } x + 6 = {}^-21$$
$$|x| = 11 \qquad\qquad \mathbf{x = 15 \text{ or } x = {}^-27}$$
$$\mathbf{x = 11 \text{ or } x = {}^-11}$$

1. $|m| - 6 = 1$

2. $3|x| + 2 = 17$

3. $5 + |x| = 23$

4. $6 + |m| - 10 = 3$

5. $^-2|a| - 6 = {}^-20$

6. $|7x - 3| = 4$

7. $|x - 10| = 6$

8. $|4n - 12| = 16$

9. $|8y + 3| = 21$

10. $5 + |2x - 1| = 8$

Solve each equation.

1. $^-8y + 3 = 35$

2. $6y + 9y = 45$

3. $4(3x + 2) = 56$

4. $20 - 2x = 30$

5. $6(3b - 2) + 5b = 57$

6. $5(m + 4) = 8(m - 2)$

7. $^-2y + 11 = 6y - 13$

8. $2p - 6 - 6p = 10 - 2p + 4$

9. $\frac{1}{2}m + \frac{1}{4} + \frac{3}{4}m = 1 + 2m$

10. $^-10 + 3|x| = 26$

11. $6 + |5y + 2| = 9$

12. $3|x + 3| = 15$

Formulas

Solve each formula for the given variable.

Example:

$$A = bh \text{ for } b$$

$$\frac{A}{h} = \frac{bh}{h}$$

$$\frac{A}{h} = b$$

1. $d = rt$ for r

2. $d = rt$ for t

3. $I = prt$ for p

4. $I = prt$ for r

5. $A = \pi r^2$ for π

6. $A = \pi r^2$ for r^2

7. $P = 2l + 2w$ for w

8. $C = 2\pi r$ for r

9. $A = \frac{1}{2}bh$ for b

10. $E = mc^2$ for m

Solving Inequalities Using Addition and Subtraction

Solve each inequality.

Example:

$$y - 6 \leq {}^-10$$
$$y \leq {}^-10 + 6$$
$$\mathbf{y \leq {}^-4}$$

1. $x + 5 > 12$

2. $y + 9 \leq {}^-12$

3. $a + 30 < 11$

4. $m - 9 \geq {}^-9$

5. $x - 15 > {}^-16$

6. $b - 2.5 \leq 6.7$

7. $m + \dfrac{1}{3} < \dfrac{4}{9}$

8. $c - \dfrac{1}{4} \geq \dfrac{1}{4}$

9. $\dfrac{2}{3} + x < \dfrac{4}{9}$

10. $5m - 4m < 21$

Solving Inequalities Using Multiplication and Division

Solve each inequality.

When multiplying or dividing by a negative number, remember to reverse the inequality symbol.

$$^-4x < 20 \qquad\qquad 5m > ^-3$$

$$\frac{^-4x}{^-4} < \frac{20}{^-4} \qquad\qquad \frac{5m}{5} > \frac{^-3}{5}$$

$$x > ^-5 \qquad\qquad m > \frac{^-3}{5}$$

1. $6x \geq ^-24$

2. $^-4m < 32$

3. $^-5y \leq ^-25$

4. $20p > ^-400$

5. $^-x < \frac{1}{2}$

6. $^-3y \geq \frac{3}{8}$

7. $9x \leq ^-6.3$

8. $27 < ^-10n + n$

Solving Multistep Inequalities

Solve each inequality.

Example:

$$6 - 8x \geq 3 - 9x$$
$$6 - 8x + 9x \geq 3$$
$$6 + x \geq 3$$
$$x \geq 3 - 6$$
$$x \geq {}^-3$$

1. $6 + 8x \leq 46$

2. ${}^-3x - 5 > 13$

3. $6 - 5y \geq 21$

4. ${}^-7x + 4 < 39$

5. $19 - 6m - 2m > 39$

6. $10a + 7 - 7a \leq {}^-6$

7. $28 - 10x > 15x - 17$

8. $43 - 14b < 14b - 13$

9. $\dfrac{3m}{5} < {}^-15$

10. $\dfrac{x}{4} + 1 \geq \dfrac{1}{4}$

Graphing Inequalities on a Number Line

Solve and graph the solution on a number line.

$x - 6 \leq {}^-7$

$x \leq {}^-1$

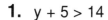

$^-1\ 0$

For $\leq$ or $\geq$ use a solid circle. For $<$ or $>$ use an open circle.

1. $y + 5 > 14$

```
◄─┼┼┼┼┼┼┼┼┼┼┼┼┼┼┼┼┼┼┼┼┼─►
 -10-9 -8 -7 -6 -5 -4 -3 -2 -1 0 1 2 3 4 5 6 7 8 9 10
```

2. $6x \leq 30$

```
◄─┼┼┼┼┼┼┼┼┼┼┼┼┼┼┼┼┼┼┼┼┼─►
 -10-9 -8 -7 -6 -5 -4 -3 -2 -1 0 1 2 3 4 5 6 7 8 9 10
```

3. $^-3y < 21$

```
◄─┼┼┼┼┼┼┼┼┼┼┼┼┼┼┼┼┼┼┼┼┼─►
 -10-9 -8 -7 -6 -5 -4 -3 -2 -1 0 1 2 3 4 5 6 7 8 9 10
```

4. $m - 5 \geq 2$

```
◄─┼┼┼┼┼┼┼┼┼┼┼┼┼┼┼┼┼┼┼┼┼─►
 -10-9 -8 -7 -6 -5 -4 -3 -2 -1 0 1 2 3 4 5 6 7 8 9 10
```

5. $3x + 5 - 2x > 11$

```
◄─┼┼┼┼┼┼┼┼┼┼┼┼┼┼┼┼┼┼┼┼┼─►
 -10-9 -8 -7 -6 -5 -4 -3 -2 -1 0 1 2 3 4 5 6 7 8 9 10
```

6. $6a + 10 < 2a - 2$

7. $^-9c - 12 \leq 42$

```
◄─┼┼┼┼┼┼┼┼┼┼┼┼┼┼┼┼┼┼┼┼┼─►
 -10-9 -8 -7 -6 -5 -4 -3 -2 -1 0 1 2 3 4 5 6 7 8 9 10
```

8. $7m + 4 \geq 25$

www.summerbridgeactivities.com   ©RBP Books

Multiplying Using Exponents

Simplify. Write using exponents.

Example:

$$6^2 \cdot 6^5 = 6^{2+5} = \mathbf{6^7}$$

$$x^2 \cdot y^3 \cdot x^2 = x^{2+2} \cdot y^3 = \mathbf{x^4 y^3}$$

1. $3^5 \cdot 3^4$

2. $9^9 \cdot 9^5 \cdot 9$

3. $(-5)^4(-5)^3$

4. $x^3 \cdot x^{10}$

5. $y^8 \cdot y^0 \cdot y^5$

6. $m \cdot m \cdot m$

7. $(x^2 y^5)(x^3 y^5)$

8. $(3a^4 b^5)(3a^2 b^3)$

9. $(b^2 c^5 d)(b^5 c d)$

10. $(2xy^3)(2x^3 y)$

11. $(mn^4)(m^5 n^6)$

12. $(xyz)(x^3 y^2 z^4)$

Algebra I Grades 5–8—RBP0105

Dividing Using Exponents

Simplify. Write using exponents.

Example:

$$\frac{5^5}{5^2} = 5^{5-2} = \mathbf{5^3}$$

$$\frac{x^6}{x} = x^{6-1} = \mathbf{x^5}$$

1. $\dfrac{6^7}{6^3}$

2. $\dfrac{4^9}{4^5}$

3. $\dfrac{n^6}{n^5}$

4. $\dfrac{x^{10}}{x^7}$

5. $\dfrac{a^4}{a}$

6. $\dfrac{m^5n^7}{mn^4}$

7. $\dfrac{a^9b}{a^8b}$

8. $\dfrac{4^4x^5}{4^3x^2}$

9. $\dfrac{x^4y^3}{xy}$

10. $\dfrac{5^2a^4b}{5a^2b}$

More with Exponents

Part I: Express using positive exponents.

$$a^{-2} = \frac{1}{a^2} \qquad\qquad xy^{-1} = x \cdot \frac{1}{y} = \frac{x}{y}$$

1. 4^{-3}

2. 5^{-4}

3. m^{-6}

4. $(3y)^{-2}$

5. $7n^{-4}$

6. cd^{-5}

Part II: Simplify.

$$(2x^3)^2 = 2^2(x^3)^2$$
$$= 4x^6$$

7. $(4^2)^2$

8. $(m^4)^8$

9. $(2t)^4$

10. $(3x^2)^3$

11. $(\frac{3}{a^2})^2$

12. $(\frac{ab^2}{c})^3$

Multiply.

Example:

$$(^-5a^2 b^3)(4ab^2) = (^-5 \cdot 4)(a^2 \cdot a)(b^3 \cdot b^2)$$
$$= {}^-20a^3b^5$$

1. $(4y)(^-3)$

2. $^-x(x)$

3. $(^-m)(^-m)$

4. $(4p^2)(2p^5)$

5. $(^-y^3)(y^5)$

6. $(^-6n^2)(^-5n^4)$

7. $(a^3b^4)(a^2b)$

8. $(^-3xy^3)(9x^3y^2)$

9. $(4m^4n)(^-4m^2n^5)$

10. $(8c^2)(2c)(^-3c^3)$

Dividing Monomials

Divide.

$$\frac{6x^4y^3}{-3x^2y} = \frac{6}{-3} \cdot x^{4-2} \cdot y^{3-1}$$

$$= {}^{-}2x^2y^2$$

1. $\dfrac{m^7}{m^4}$

2. $\dfrac{12x^2}{8x}$

3. $\dfrac{b^6}{b}$

4. $\dfrac{4c^3}{c^6}$

5. $\dfrac{{}^{-}8x^{10}}{2x^5}$

6. $\dfrac{16y^2}{{}^{-}4y^2}$

7. $\dfrac{{}^{-}35m^5}{{}^{-}35}$

8. $\dfrac{32x^6y^8}{{}^{-}4x^6y^3}$

9. $\dfrac{5m^{10}n^6}{{}^{-}7m^5n^2}$

10. $\dfrac{36a^6b^3}{{}^{-}9ab^3}$

Simplify.

Example:

$$4a^5b^3 + 3ab^2 - 2a^5b^3 - 5ab^2$$
$$= (4 - 2)a^5b^3 + (3 - 5)ab^2$$
$$= \mathbf{2a^5b^3 - 2ab^2}$$

1. $2y - 5y^3 - 32 - 8y^3$

2. $8n^3 - n - n^3 - 8$

3. $6y^2 + 5y^2 - 4$

4. $4c^4 - 2c + 2c + c^4$

5. $7x^3 + 6xy^2 - 2x^3 - 3xy^2$

6. $^-9a^2b^2 + 3ab - 6a^2b^2 - 5ab$

7. $3xy^2 + 4xy - 10xy^2 + xy$

8. $3m^2n^2 - m^2 + m^3 - 2 - 2m^2n^2$

9. $4x^2y + xy - 4x^2y - xy + 3x^2y$

Adding Polynomials

Add.

$$(2x^3 - 3x - 5) + (4x^3 - 2x^2 + 3)$$
$$= 2x^3 - 3x - 5 + 4x^3 - 2x^2 + 3$$
$$= \mathbf{6x^3 - 2x^2 - 3x - 2}$$

1. $(^-2a^2 + 5a) + (3a^2 + a)$

2. $(32y^4 + y^2 + 3y) + (3y^2 - 2y)$

3. $(4m^5 + 7m^2 - 1) + (6m^2 + 5m - 2)$

4. $(^-5x^3 + 7x^2 - 2x - 1) + (4x^3 + 3x - 9)$

5. $(10x^7 - 8x^4 + 3x^2 + 2) + (6x^5 - 2x^4 + 5x^2)$

6. $(^-2a^2b^2 + ab + 5) + (5b^3 - 5a^2b^2 + 3ab - 2)$

7. $(2y^3 - 3x^2y^4 + 3x) + (^-4y^3 + 3x^2 - 5x + 6)$

8. $(^-2m^4n^3 + 7m^3n^3 - 5m^2 + 2mn^2 + 3) + (^-m^3n^3 + 3m^2 + 6)$

9. $(2x^2y - 4xy + 8) + (8xy^2 - 3x^2y + xy - 10)$

Algebra I Grades 5–8—RBP0105

Subtract.

Example:

$(8y^2 + 6) - (5y^2 + 2)$
$= 8y^2 + 6 - 5y^2 - 2$
$= \mathbf{3y^2 + 4}$

1. $(4a^4 + 5) - (2a^4 - 1)$

2. $(^-5x^3 + 3x + 7) - (^-4x^2 - 5)$

3. $(8y^3 - 3y + 9) - (8y^2 + 2y - 7)$

4. $9m^3 - (^-3m^2 - 2m + 1)$

5. $(6x^4 - 2x^3 + 3x + 1) - (3x^3 - 2x + 5)$

6. $(6t^4 + 5t) - (5t^5 - 2t^4 + 3t^2 + 2t - 1)$

7. $(y^4 - 2y^2 + y + 1) - (y^4 - 3y^3 + 3y - 1)$

8. $(5n^5 + 2n^3 + 6n - 3) - (4n^5 - 5n^4 - 8n - 6)$

9. $(6ab^5 + b^4 - 4ab^3 + 2b^2) - (^-ab^5 - ab^4 - b^2 - 1)$

Multiplying Monomials

Multiply.

Example: $3x(4x + 5) = (3x)(4x) + (3x)(5)$
$$= 12x^2 + 15x$$

1. $6c(5c + 3)$

2. $4m^2(^-3m^3 + 2)$

3. $^-5x^2(^-3x + 1)$

4. $^-m^2(6m^2 + n)$

5. $2y(4y^2 + 5y - 2)$

6. $^-4a(^-3a^2 + 2a - 5)$

7. $3x^5(x^4 - 2x^3 - x)$

8. $^-2n^3(n^4 + 2n^3 - n^2 - n)$

9. $3a^2(^-a^2b + b^2 - 6ab)$

10. $5x(^-y^4 - xy^2 + 5x)$

Multiply.

Example:

$$(x + 6)(x + 3) = \overset{\text{First}}{x \cdot x} + \overset{\text{Outside}}{x \cdot 3} + \overset{\text{Inside}}{6 \cdot x} + \overset{\text{Last}}{6 \cdot 3}$$
$$= x^2 + 3x + 6x + 18$$
$$= \mathbf{x^2 + 9x + 18}$$

FOIL method $\longrightarrow$ First   Outside   Inside   Last

1. $(x + 3)(x - 3)$ **2.** $(x + 4)(x - 3)$

3. $(2x + 2)(x + 4)$ **4.** $(2a + 3)(4a + 2)$

5. $(x^2 + 2)(x + 1)$ **6.** $(3b + 4)(3b - 4)$

7. $(y^3 - 3)(y + 2)$ **8.** $(5x^2 + 4)(x - 4)$

9. $(4x^3 + x^2)(x^2 + x)$ **10.** $(3x^5 + 2x^2)(x^4 + 3x)$

Multiplying Polynomials

Multiply.

$$(x - 2)(x^2 + x - 3)$$
$$= x(x^2 + x - 3) - 2(x^2 + x - 3)$$
$$= x^3 + x^2 - 3x - 2x^2 - 2x + 6$$
$$= \mathbf{x^3 - x^2 - 5x + 6}$$

1. $(m + 1)(m^2 - m + 3)$

2. $(2a - 1)(3a^2 - 2a - 1)$

3. $(x^2 - 3)(3x^2 - 4x + 2)$

4. $(n^3 - n^2)(n^3 - n^2 - n)$

5. $(x^2 - 2x + 1)(x^2 + x + 1)$

6. $(3m^3 - m^2 - 4)(3m^2 + 2m^2 + 5)$

7. $(2y^2 + y - 3)(^{-}2y^2 + 3y + 5)$

8. $(x - 1)(x^3 + x^2 + x + 1)$

   Algebra I Grades 5–8—RBP0105

Factoring Polynomials

Factor.

Example:

$$20x^3y^2 + 12xy^2 = 4xy^2(5x^2) + 4xy^2(3)$$
$$= \mathbf{4xy^2(5x^2 + 3)}$$

The common factor, $4xy^2$, was factored out.

1. $y^2 + 5y$

2. $4x^2 - 4x$

3. $17m^4 + 51m^3$

4. $4n^2 - 4n + 16$

5. $6x^2y + 3x^2y^2$

6. $5m^4n^4 - 3m^3n + 30n^3$

7. $a^9 + a^7 - a^4 - a^2 + a$

8. $5x^3y^2 - 15xy^3 + 20x^2y^2 - xy^2$

Factor.

Example:

$x^2 + 8x + 16 = (x + 4)^2$

A trinomial square, such as $x^2 + 8x + 16$, is the square of a binomial, $(x + 4)^2$.

1. $x^2 - 10x + 25$

2. $x^2 + 16x + 64$

3. $x^2 + 6x + 9$

4. $x^2 + 14x + 49$

5. $x^2 - 2x + 1$

6. $a^2 + 6ab + 9b^2$

7. $16x^2 - 40xy + 25y^2$

8. $9x^2 - 30x + 25$

9. $4x^4 + 16x^2 + 16$

10. $9x^4 - 6x^2y + y^2$

Factor.

Example:

$$x^2 + 7x + 12 = (x + 3)(x + 4)$$
$$2x^2 - 22x + 60 = 2(x - 5)(x - 6)$$

1. $x^2 - 8x + 15$

2. $x^2 + 10x + 24$

3. $x^2 - 4x - 45$

4. $x^2 + 11x + 28$

5. $x^2 - 14x + 45$

6. $x^2 + 10x + 21$

7. $x^2 - 21x - 100$

8. $2x^2 + 8x + 8$

9. $3x^2 - x - 4$

10. $4x^2 + 4x - 15$

www.summerbridgeactivities.com   ©RBP Books

Solve for x.

Example:

$$x^2 + x = 42$$
$$x^2 + x - 42 = 0$$
$$(x - 7)(x + 6) = 0$$
$$x - 7 = 0 \text{ or } x + 6 = 0$$
$$\mathbf{x = 7 \text{ or } x = ^-6}$$

1. $x^2 - 3x - 28 = 0$

2. $x^2 + x - 12 = 0$

3. $x^2 + 6x - 27 = 0$

4. $x^2 + 5x = ^-6$

5. $x^2 - 9x = ^-14$

6. $2x^2 + 25x + 72 = 0$

7. $3x^2 = 27$

8. $3w^2 + 5w = ^-2$

9. $6x^2 = 4x$

10. $3x^2 - 2x = 5$

Simplify.

Example:

$$\frac{3x}{3x^2 + 3x} = \frac{3x}{3x(x + 1)} = \frac{1}{x + 1}$$

1. $\dfrac{6x + 24}{48x}$

2. $\dfrac{5y - 10}{5y}$

3. $\dfrac{3m - 12}{3m}$

4. $\dfrac{x^5 - x^4}{x^4 - x^3}$

5. $\dfrac{x + 8}{x^2 - 64}$

6. $\dfrac{x^2 - 1}{x + 1}$

7. $\dfrac{5x + 5}{x^2 + 7x + 6}$

8. $\dfrac{3x - 15}{5 - x}$

9. $\dfrac{x^2 - 1}{2x^2 - x - 1}$

10. $\dfrac{4x - 12}{6 - 2x}$

Multiply. Simplify the product.

Example:

$$\frac{^-3}{3x + 6} \cdot \frac{2}{x - 4} = \frac{^-3 \cdot 2}{(3x + 6)(x - 4)}$$

$$= \frac{^-3 \cdot 2}{3(x + 2)(x - 4)}$$

$$= \frac{^-2}{(x + 2)(x - 4)}$$

1. $\dfrac{5a^2}{2} \cdot \dfrac{6}{10a^2}$

2. $\dfrac{3a}{b^2} \cdot \dfrac{4b}{9a^2}$

3. $\dfrac{x + 5}{2x} \cdot \dfrac{4x^3}{x + 5}$

4. $\dfrac{^-3}{c} \cdot \dfrac{c^5}{c + 3}$

5. $\dfrac{x + 3}{x^2 - 2} \cdot \dfrac{x + 3}{x^2 - 9}$

6. $\dfrac{x - 3}{x - 4} \cdot \dfrac{x + 4}{x - 3}$

7. $\dfrac{4(x - 1)}{(x + 2)^2} \cdot \dfrac{x + 2}{(x - 1)^2}$

8. $\dfrac{x^2}{x^2 - 4} \cdot \dfrac{x^2 - 5x + 6}{x^2 - 3x}$

Algebra I Grades 5–8—RBP0105

Dividing Rational Expressions

Divide. Simplify the quotient.

Example:

$$\frac{2x + 8}{6} \div \frac{x + 4}{12} = \frac{2x + 8}{6} \cdot \frac{12}{x + 4}$$

$$= \frac{2(x + 4)(12)}{6(x + 4)}$$

$$= 4$$

1. $\dfrac{3x^2}{8} \div \dfrac{6x}{5}$

2. $\dfrac{3}{x^5} \div \dfrac{9}{x^4}$

3. $\dfrac{6x^3}{7} \div 2x$

4. $\dfrac{4x - 4}{18} \div \dfrac{x - 1}{3}$

5. $\dfrac{4x - 8}{15} \div \dfrac{x - 2}{10}$

6. $\dfrac{x^2 - 1}{x} \div \dfrac{x - 1}{x + 1}$

7. $\dfrac{x^2 - 5x + 6}{x - 3} \div (x - 2)$

8. $\dfrac{x^2 - x - 20}{x^2 + 7 + 12} \div \dfrac{x^2 - 7x + 10}{x^2 + 10x + 24}$

Adding and Subtracting Rational Expressions

Add or subtract. Simplify.

Example:

$$\frac{x+5}{x+6} - \frac{3x-7}{x+6} = \frac{x+5-(3x-7)}{x+6}$$

$$= \frac{x+5-3x+7}{x+6}$$

$$= \frac{{}^-2x+12}{x+6}$$

$$= \frac{{}^-2(x+6)}{x+6}$$

$$= {}^-2$$

1. $\dfrac{10m}{y} - \dfrac{8m}{y}$

2. $\dfrac{{}^-5x}{x-6} + \dfrac{x-12}{x-6}$

3. $\dfrac{x+4}{2x+2} - \dfrac{3x}{2x+2}$

4. $\dfrac{x+6}{x+3} - \dfrac{{}^-3x-6}{x+3}$

5. $\dfrac{5a^2-3a+2}{2a-1} - \dfrac{3a^2+3a-2}{2a-1}$

6. $\dfrac{2x^2-13x-8}{x+4} + \dfrac{x^2+3x}{x+4}$

7. $\dfrac{x^2-3x}{2x+1} - \dfrac{3x^2+4x}{2x+1}$

8. $\dfrac{{}^-3x^2+2x+4}{5x+1} + \dfrac{4x^2+2x-3}{5x+1}$

Solving Rational Equations

Solve each equation.

Example:

$$x - \frac{5}{x} = {}^-4$$

Multiply both sides by x, the LCM.

$$x\left(x - \frac{5}{x}\right) = {}^-4(x)$$

$$x^2 - 5 = {}^-4x$$

$$x^2 + 4x - 5 = 0$$

$$(x + 5)(x - 1) = 0$$

$$x + 5 = 0 \text{ or } x - 1 = 0$$

$$\mathbf{x = {}^-5 \text{ or } x = 1}$$

1. $c + \dfrac{3}{c} = {}^-4$

2. $\dfrac{1}{6} + \dfrac{1}{5} = \dfrac{1}{x}$

3. $\dfrac{5}{b} + \dfrac{1}{2} = \dfrac{4}{b}$

4. $\dfrac{1}{6-y} = \dfrac{1}{y}$

5. $\dfrac{3}{a+2} = \dfrac{5}{a-1}$

6. $\dfrac{x-3}{3x+2} = \dfrac{1}{5}$

7. $\dfrac{3x+1}{3x-2} = \dfrac{2x-3}{2x+2}$

8. $\dfrac{a-1}{a+1} = \dfrac{a-2}{a-3}$

Simplify.

Example:

$$\sqrt{x^2} = |x|$$

$$\sqrt{x^{12}} = \sqrt{(x^6)^2} = x^6$$

$$\sqrt{9x^5} = \sqrt{3 \cdot 3 \cdot x^2 \cdot x^2 \cdot x}$$

$$= 3x^2 \sqrt{x}$$

1. $\sqrt{16x^2}$

2. $\sqrt{(x-4)^2}$

3. $\sqrt{x^{10}}$

4. $\sqrt{x^{14}}$

5. $\sqrt{x^{15}}$

6. $\sqrt{25(x+5)^6}$

7. $\sqrt{12x^7}$

8. $\sqrt{225x^4y^3}$

9. $\sqrt{36x^5y^8}$

10. $\sqrt{(x+2)^{10}}$

Multiply and simplify.

$$\sqrt{3} \cdot \sqrt{27} = \sqrt{3 \cdot 27} \qquad \sqrt{5x} \cdot \sqrt{20x^2} = \sqrt{5x \cdot 20x^2}$$
$$= \sqrt{81} \qquad\qquad\qquad = \sqrt{100x^3}$$
$$= \pm 9 \qquad\qquad\qquad = \pm 10x\sqrt{x}$$

1. $\sqrt{5} \cdot \sqrt{15}$

2. $\sqrt{6} \cdot \sqrt{18x}$

3. $\sqrt{2x} \cdot \sqrt{18y}$

4. $\sqrt{7x} \cdot \sqrt{35y}$

5. $\sqrt{5} \cdot \sqrt{4x + 2}$

6. $\sqrt{2x^3} \cdot \sqrt{6x^3y^6}$

7. $\sqrt{5x^2y} \cdot \sqrt{10xy^2}$

8. $\sqrt{ab} \cdot \sqrt{ac}$

9. $\sqrt{x^{215}} \cdot \sqrt{y^{29}}$

10. $\sqrt{(x + 5)^6} \cdot \sqrt{(x + 5)^9}$

Dividing Radical Expressions

Divide and simplify.

Example:

$$\frac{\sqrt{21}}{\sqrt{7}} = \sqrt{\frac{21}{7}} = \sqrt{3}$$

$$\frac{8}{\sqrt{2}} = \frac{8}{\sqrt{2}} \cdot \frac{\sqrt{2}}{\sqrt{2}}$$

$$= \frac{8\sqrt{2}}{2}$$

$$= 4\sqrt{2}$$

1. $\dfrac{\sqrt{16}}{\sqrt{25}}$

2. $\dfrac{\sqrt{1}}{\sqrt{4}}$

3. $\dfrac{\sqrt{18}}{\sqrt{3}}$

4. $\dfrac{\sqrt{15x^7}}{\sqrt{5x}}$

5. $\dfrac{\sqrt{45x^3}}{\sqrt{5x}}$

6. $\dfrac{2}{\sqrt{2}}$

7. $\dfrac{\sqrt{4}}{\sqrt{x}}$

8. $\dfrac{6x}{\sqrt{5}}$

Add or subtract.

Example:

$$2\sqrt{7} + 3\sqrt{7} = (2+3)\sqrt{7}$$
$$= 5\sqrt{7}$$

$$\sqrt{27} - \sqrt{3} = \sqrt{9 \cdot 3} - \sqrt{3}$$
$$= 3\sqrt{3} - \sqrt{3}$$
$$= 2\sqrt{3}$$

1. $3\sqrt{5} + 4\sqrt{5}$

2. $9\sqrt{2} - 5\sqrt{2}$

3. $8\sqrt{x} + 4\sqrt{x}$

4. $6\sqrt{8} + 2\sqrt{2}$

5. $\sqrt{20} + \sqrt{45}$

6. $\sqrt{80} - \sqrt{45}$

7. $\sqrt{4x} + \sqrt{9x^5}$

8. $\sqrt{8x+8} + \sqrt{2x+2}$

9. $\sqrt{x^9 - x^6} + \sqrt{4x^3 - 4}$

10. $\sqrt{3} - \sqrt{\frac{1}{3}}$

Solve.

Example:

$$\sqrt{2x} - 5 = 9$$

$$\sqrt{2x} = 14$$

$$(\sqrt{2x})^2 = (14)^2$$

$$2x = 196$$

$$\mathbf{x = 98}$$

1. $\sqrt{x} = 11$

2. $\sqrt{x} = 5.2$

3. $\sqrt{3x} - 6 = 2$

4. $\sqrt{x + 4} = 20$

5. $\sqrt{2x + 1} = 13$

6. $4 + \sqrt{x - 1} = 6$

7. $\sqrt{7x - 6} = \sqrt{x + 12}$

8. $\sqrt{5x - 4} = \sqrt{x + 16}$

Algebra I Grades 5–8—RBP0105

Solve.

Example:

$$x^2 + 6x = 0$$
$$x(x + 6) = 0$$
$$x = 0 \text{ or } x + 6 = 0$$
$$\mathbf{x = 0} \text{ or } \mathbf{x = {}^-6}$$

$$x^2 - 2x - 8 = 0$$
$$(x - 4)(x + 2) = 0$$
$$x - 4 = 0 \text{ or } x + 2 = 0$$
$$\mathbf{x = 4} \text{ or } \mathbf{x = {}^-2}$$

1. $x^2 + 7x = 0$

2. $4x^2 + 8x = 0$

3. $7x^2 - 3x = 0$

4. $5x^2 + 5x = 0$

5. $x^2 + 7x + 6 = 0$

6. $x^2 - 2x - 48 = 0$

7. $x^2 + 6x = {}^-9$

8. $3x^2 + 18x = {}^-15$

Solving Quadratic Equations by Completing the Square

Solve by completing the square.

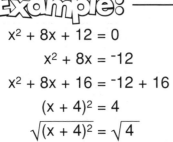

Example:

$x^2 + 8x + 12 = 0$

$x^2 + 8x = {}^-12$

$x^2 + 8x + 16 = {}^-12 + 16$

$(x + 4)^2 = 4$

$\sqrt{(x + 4)^2} = \sqrt{4}$

$x + 4 = 2$ or $x + 4 = {}^-2$

$\mathbf{x = {}^-2}$ or $\mathbf{x = {}^-6}$

To complete the square, take half of the x coefficient, square it, and add it to both sides.

Tip: Make sure the coefficient of x^2 is 1.

1. $x^2 + 14x = 15$

2. $x^2 - 7x - 2 = 0$

3. $x^2 + 8x + 15 = 0$

4. $x^2 - 2x - 10 = 0$

5. $x^2 + 2x - 5 = 0$

6. $2x^2 - 9x - 5 = 0$

7. $3x^2 - 2x - 5 = 0$

8. $6x^2 + 11x = 10$

Solve by using the quadratic formula.

Example:

$$2x^2 + 7x = 4$$

$$2x^2 + 7x - 4 = 0$$

$$a = 2 \quad b = 7 \quad c = ^-4$$

The Quadratic Formula
$x = \dfrac{^-b \pm \sqrt{b^2 - 4ac}}{2a}$

$$x = \frac{^-7 \pm \sqrt{7^2 - (4 \cdot 2 \cdot ^-4)}}{2 \cdot 2}$$

$$x = \frac{^-7 \pm \sqrt{49 + 32}}{4}$$

$$x = \frac{^-7 + \sqrt{81}}{4} \text{ or } x = \frac{^-7 - \sqrt{81}}{4}$$

$$x = \frac{2}{4} \text{ or } x = \frac{^-16}{4}$$

$$\mathbf{x = \tfrac{1}{2} \text{ or } x = ^-4}$$

1. $x^2 - 10x = ^-22$

2. $3x^2 - 2x = 8$

3. $2x^2 + 5 = ^-6x$

4. $2x^2 - 5x - 1 = 0$

Graphing Ordered Pairs

Plot the following points. The first one has been done for you.

1. A (-3,4)

2. B (5,0)

3. C (3,-2)

4. D (0,5)

5. E (-3,-4)

6. F (0,-3)

7. G (-1,1)

8. H (-4,0)

9. I (5,5)

10. J (3,2)

Algebra I Grades 5–8—RBP0105

Graph each linear equation using three points.

 **:**

$$3x + y = 2$$
$$y = {}^-3x + 2$$

x	y
0	2
⁻1	5
1	-1

1. Solve for y.
2. Substitute 0, ⁻1, and 1 for x and find the corresponding values for y to make an ordered pair.

1. $y = x - 1$

2. $y = 2x + 1$

3. $y = {}^-5x + 1$

4. $y - 4 = 3x$

5. $8x - 4y = 12$

6. $3y - 6 = 9x$

www.summerbridgeactivities.com   ©RBP Books

Graphing Using Intercepts

Graph each linear equation using the x- and y-intercepts.

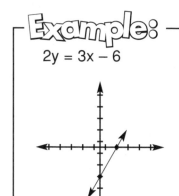

Example:

2y = 3x − 6

y-intercept	x-intercept
2y = 3(0) − 6	2(0) = 3x − 6
2y = ⁻6	6 = 3x
y = ⁻3	x = 2
(0,⁻3)	(2,0)

1. x − 2 = y

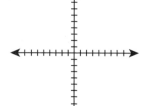

2. 3x + 1 = y

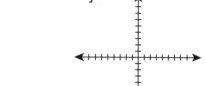

3. 4x − 3y = 12

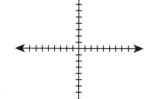

4. ⁻4x + y = 2

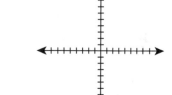

5. y = ⁻2 − 2x

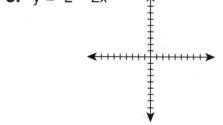

6. 3y = 2x + 4

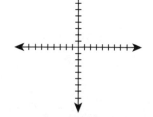

Algebra I Grades 5–8—RBP0105

Slope

Given two points, find the slope of each line.

Example:

Slope: steepness of line = $\dfrac{\text{change in y}}{\text{change in x}}$

$$(^-5,2), (4,^-1) = \dfrac{^-1 - 2}{4 - (^-5)} = \dfrac{^-3}{9} = \dfrac{^-1}{3}$$

1. (5,7), (4,0)

2. (2,1), (6,2)

3. (^-1,7), (^-4,9)

4. (1,10), (5,8)

5. (4,^-1), (6,^-5)

6. (^-3,3), (5,^-8)

7. (0,0), (^-2,^-8)

8. (2,7), (^-3,^-5)

www.summerbridgeactivities.com

Graphing Using the Slope-Intercept Equation

Graph each linear equation using the y-intercept and slope.

Example:

Slope-intercept equation: y = mx + b, where
m = slope and b = y-intercept.

y = 2x − 5

y-intercept: (0,⁻5)
slope: 2

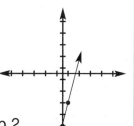

From the intercept, use the slope, $\frac{2}{1}$, to go up 2
and to the right 1 to get the second point.

1. y = ⁻3x + 7

2. y = 2x − 4

3. y = ⁻4x − 2

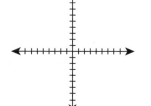

4. y + 3 = ⁻x

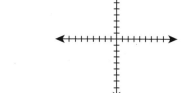

5. 2x + 3y = 6

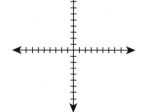

6. y + $\frac{2}{5}$x = ⁻2

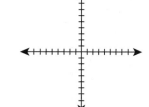

Algebra I Grades 5–8—RBP0105

The Slope-Intercept Equation

Write an equation for each line that contains the given point and has the given slope.

Example:

(3,6), m = 1

6 = 1(3) + b

6 = 3 + b

b = 3

Slope-intercept equation:
y = mx + b, where m = slope and b = y-intercept.

Find b by substituting the point and slope into the equation.

y = x + 3

1. (-3,0), m = -2

2. (3,5), m = 6

3. (0,3), m = -3

4. (-2,1), m = 3

5. (-2,4), m = $-\frac{1}{2}$

6. (-2,1), m = $\frac{1}{2}$

The Point-Slope Equation

Write an equation for each line that contains the given pair of points.

Point-slope equation: $y - y_1 = m(x - x_1)$, where m = slope and (x_1, y_1) = a point on the line.

$$(^-3, ^-2), (^-1, 4)$$

$$\text{Slope} = \frac{4 - (^-2)}{^-1 - (^-3)}$$

$$= \frac{6}{2}$$

$$= 3$$

$$y - 4 = 3(x - (^-1))$$

$$y - 4 = 3x + 3$$

$$\mathbf{y = 3x + 7}$$

1. (2,3), (⁻5,1)

2. (1,5), (3,2)

3. (0,0), (6,3)

4. (4,0), (0,⁻2)

5. (⁻2,6), (4,2)

6. (⁻4,0), (0,6)

Solving Systems of Equations: Graphing

Solve by graphing.

$$y = 2x + 1$$
$$y + x = 4$$

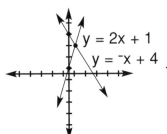

1. Graph both lines on the same graph.
2. Their intersection is the solution.

The solution is **(1,3)**.

1. $y = {}^-2x + 5$
   $2y = 5x + 10$

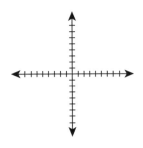

2. $x = y$
   $2x = y - 3$

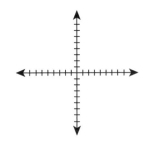

3. $x - 2y = 6$
   $2x - 3y = 5$

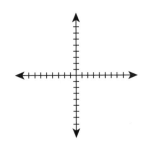

4. $y = 2x + 8$
   $y - 2x = 7$

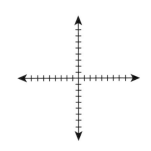

Solving Systems of Equations:
The Substitution Method

Solve by using the substitution method.

$y = 2x - 1$

$y = x + 2$

Substitute $2x - 1$ for y in the second equation. Solve for x. Plug x into either equation to solve for y.

$2x - 1 = x + 2$

$x = 3$

$y = 3 + 2$

$y = 5$

The solution is **(3,5)**.

1. $y = {}^-2x + 8$
$y = x + 5$

2. $y = {}^-4x - 5$
$y = {}^-2x + 10$

3. $x + y = {}^-2$
$x - y = 6$

4. $4x - 3y = 15$
$x - 2y = 0$

5. ${}^-2y + x = 8$
$3y + 2x = 2$

6. $4x = 3 - y$
$8x + 2y = 6$

Solving Systems of Equations: The Addition Method

Solve by using the addition method.

Example:

$$3x + 5y = {}^-2$$
$$8x - 5y = {}^-9$$

$$
\begin{array}{r}
3x + 5y = {}^-2 \\
+\ 8x - 5y = {}^-9 \\
\hline
11x = {}^-11 \\
x = {}^-1
\end{array}
$$

Plug $x = {}^-1$ into either equation to find y.

$$3({}^-1) + 5y = {}^-2$$
$${}^-3 + 5y = {}^-2$$
$$5y = 1$$
$$y = \frac{1}{5}$$

The solution is $({}^-1, \frac{1}{5})$.

1. $x + y = 3$
$x - y = 7$

2. ${}^-x + 2y = 7$
$x + y = 8$

3. $x - 5y = {}^-2$
$7x + 5y = 18$

4. $4x + 3y = 7$
${}^-4x + y = 5$

5. $5x - 2y = {}^-3$
$5x + 3y = 17$

6. $2x - 3y = {}^-11$
$5x - 2y = 0$

Linear Inequalities

Graph on a coordinate plane.

Example:

y ≤ x + 4

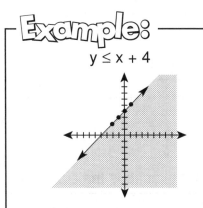

1. Graph the linear equation
   y = x + 4.
2. Use a solid line for ≤ or ≥ and
   a dashed line for < or >.
3. Shade the half-plane that
   makes the inequality true.

1. y > -x – 2

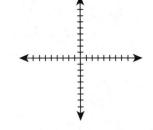

2. y ≥ x – 4

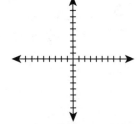

3. y ≤ ⁻2x + 4

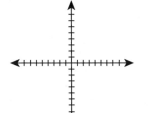

4. x > 3

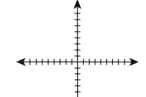

5. y + 3x < 0

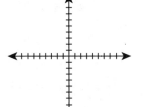

6. y ≥ 2 – 2x

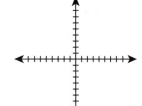

Graphing Systems of Linear Inequalities

Solve these systems by graphing.

Example:

$$y > x + 2$$
$$y > 3$$

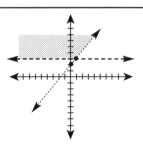

The region where the solutions (shading) overlap is the solution.

1. $y > 3x - 1$
   $y < {}^-2x + 3$

2. $y < 4x + 2$
   $y \geq {}^-x + 1$

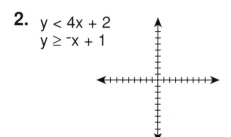

3. $y > 5$
   $2y > {}^-x + 4$

4. $x + y \leq 4$
   $y - x > 5$

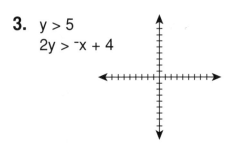

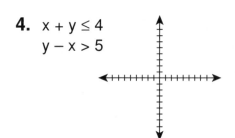

5. $x + 2y \geq 6$
   $3x + 3y < 12$

6. $3x - y > 4$
   $x + y < {}^-1$

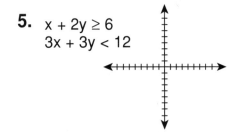

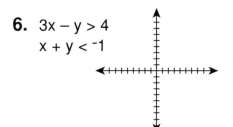

www.summerbridgeactivities.com   © RBP Books

Using Equations

Solve by using an equation.

1. Maria earned $2,300 more her second year on the job than her first. If she earned $29,100 her second year, what did she earn her first?

2. The dryers at the local laundromat cost 1 quarter for every 7 minutes. How many quarters will Burt have to use to dry 2 loads of laundry if each load takes 50 minutes to dry?

3. Jenny earned x amount of dollars babysitting Friday night. On Saturday night, she earned twice as much. If she earned $36 for both nights, how much did she earn the first night?

4. An artist sells each of his paintings for $50 at a craft show. How many did he sell at the show if he earned $1,850?

5. A roll of film costs $4.99. Each print costs $0.30 to develop. What is the total cost involved in buying and developing a roll of 36 exposures?

Algebra I Grades 5–8—RBP0105

Using Proportions

Solve by using a proportion.

1. A car travels 310 miles on 13 gallons of gasoline. How many gallons are needed to drive 475 miles?

2. A museum has a policy that 2 adults must accompany every group of 8 students. How many adults are needed to bring 120 students to the museum?

3. The ratio of non-American born students to American born students at a school is 7 to 25. How many non-American born students attend this school if 425 are American born?

4. The scale on a map is 1 cm: 4.2 km. If there are 12.5 cm between two cities on the map, what is the actual distance between the two cities?

5. The ratio of girls to boys in a school is 3:5. If there are 220 boys, what is the total number of students in the school?

6. It takes Bruce twelve minutes to type two-thirds of a page. He is typing a seven-page term paper. If he continues at his present rate, how long total will it take him to finish his paper?

©RBP Books

Make a Table

Solve by making a table.

1. A wealthy man donated money to his alma mater for a 10-year period. The first year he gave $1 million. The second year he gave $3 million. The third year he gave $5 million and so on. How much money did he give in all for the 10 years?

2. Shanika was offered two jobs when she graduated from college. One job had a starting salary of $19,000, with a guaranteed pay raise of $3,000 each year for 10 years. The other job had a starting salary of $27,000, with a guaranteed pay raise of $2,000 each year for 10 years. After 10 years which job would be paying more?

3. XYZ Company needs to expand their personnel due to record sales. In week number one, each of the original 25 employees hires and trains 2 new people. In week two, each of the new people hires and trains 2 new people. In week three, each of the newest employees hires and trains 2 new people. If the company continues this hiring trend over the next two months (eight weeks), how many employees will it have?

4. Stanley bought a car for $29,000. If it loses 10% of its value each year, what is the value of the car after 4 years?

Algebra I Grades 5–8—RBP0105

Quantitative Comparisons

Compare the quantities in Column A with those in Column B, and choose from one of the four statements below.

(A) The quantity in column A is greater.
(B) The quantity in column B is greater.
(C) The two quantities are equal.
(D) The relationship cannot be determined.

	Column A	If...	Column B
1.	$(a + 2)(a + 3)$	$a > 0$	$(a + 2)^2$
2.	$\frac{1}{2}x$		$0.5x$
3.	x	$x < y < 0$	$-3y$
4.	xy	$x < y < z$	y^2
5.	$4.0 \times 6{,}545$		$4.1 \times 6{,}545$
6.	$a + b$	$ab > 0$	$a - b$
7.	$\dfrac{a}{b}$	$b > 1$ $a < 0$	ab

Working Backwards

Solve each problem.

1. Aimee is thinking of a number. She divides her number by 8, squares it, then cuts it in thirds. Her result is 12. What number was Aimee thinking of?

2. Juan is thinking of a number. He halves it and then multiplies the result by itself. He now has 2,401. What number was Juan thinking of?

3. Keri bought a new pack of graph paper for math class. When she got to class and opened it up, three people asked her for some. She gave one quarter of the pack to Christopher. Alyson got one fourth of what was left. Then Mark took one third of the remainder. That left Keri with 36 sheets. How many sheets were in the pack of graph paper?

4. Michael is tall. Add 20 centimeters to his height and take a third of the sum. That gives you half of Ranaan's height. Ranaan is 150 centimeters tall. How tall is Michael?

5. Angel bought a pair of jeans at a one-third-off sale. Angel spent $14.30 for them. What was the original price of the jeans?

Using Logical Reasoning

Solve each problem.

1. Without computing, find the number that is the cube of 93:

   a. 804,958   b. 805,643

   c. 804,357   d. 804,872

2. It takes Millie about 4 minutes to saw through a log. How long will it take her to saw the log into 4 pieces?

3. A company hired Ronnie and Kenny as consultants. Together they made $14,500. If Ronnie had earned $500 less, both he and Kenny would have been paid the same. How much were they each paid?

4. Five boys in a race finished within 8 seconds of each other. Ricky finished 1 second ahead of Craig, and Craig was not last. Sam finished 6 seconds before Taylor. Taylor finished 3 seconds behind Ricky. Ricky finished 5 seconds behind Bob. In what order did the boys finish?

5. Rachel, Robert, Charla, and Kenneth were hired by the local rec league as coaches. Basketball, tennis, volleyball, and racquetball were the coaching positions. Robert's sister was hired to coach tennis. Neither Robert nor Kenneth ever played volleyball or knew how to coach it. Charla had never learned to play tennis. Kenneth disliked all sports that involved the use of a racket. Who was hired to coach which sport?

Using a Formula

Solve each problem.

1. A conference room is 20 feet long by 15 feet wide. Find the maximum amount of carpeting needed to cover the room's floor.

2. Find the distance you travel if you drive your car at an average speed of 55 mph for 8 hours. Use the formula d = rt where *d* is distance, *r* is rate, and *t* is time.

3. How much profit does Jake make on a big screen television set that sells for $2,199 if it cost him $1,099, and he paid the salesperson that sold it a commission of $250? Use the formula P = I – E where *P* is profit, *I* is income, and *E* is expense.

4. Two buses leave town at the same time going in opposite directions. One bus travels at 48 mph, and the other travels at 55 mph. In how many hours will they be 206 miles apart? Use the formula d = rt.

5. An airplane took 2 hours to fly 600 miles against a head wind. The return trip with the wind took $1\frac{2}{3}$ hours. Find the speed of the plane in the still air.

Algebra I Grades 5–8—RBP0105

Using Percent

Solve each problem.

1. Anita's math test had 42 problems. She answered 37 correctly. What percent of the problems did she answer correctly?

2. A softball player had 40 hits in 150 times at bat for the season. What percent of her times at bat were hits?

3. The sales tax rate in Larry's hometown is 7%. How much tax would be charged on a purchase of $521.95? How much will the total cost of the purchase be?

4. Tanya's meal came to $21.04. Calculate a 7% sales tax, and then calculate a 15% tip based on the cost of the meal only. Including tax and tip, how much did Tanya's meal cost?

5. Which is better, a discount of 20% or successive discounts of 10% and 10%?

Answer Pages

Page 1
1. 125   2. 21   3. 96   4. 7,776
5. 3   6. 248   7. 80   8. 30
9. 100   10. 4

Page 2
1. 76   2. 75   3. 100   4. 1   5. 180
6. 1   7. $1\frac{1}{2}$ 8. 41   9. 2   10. 13

Page 3
1. $x + 5$ 2. $5 - c$ 3. $10 + p$
4. $3h$ 5. $\frac{y}{2}$ 6. $3n$
7. $n + 3x$ 8. $y + y$ or $2y$ 9. $2x - 3$
10. $6y + 2$ 11. $\frac{n}{10}$ 12. $4s$

Page 4
1. $x = 7.2$ 2. $m = 349$ 3. $a = 113$
4. $x = 287$ 5. $c = 1.64$ 6. $y = 4,946$
7. $a = \frac{4}{7}$ 8. $p = \frac{13}{15}$ 9. $x = 4.66$
10. $y = 284$

Page 5
1. $m = 7$ 2. $c = 6$ 3. $x = 0.66$
4. $m = 372$ 5. $p = 61$ 6. $a = 16$
7. $x = 236$ 8. $r = 0.96$ 9. $y = 5$
10. $m = 0.4$

Page 6
1. $7n = 63; n = 9$
2. $60h = 42,720; h = 712$ hours
3. $12b = 5; b =$ about $0.42
4. $t - 12 = 75; t = 87$ points
5. $324/2 = w; w = 162$ white golf balls
6. $56.25 + x = 70; x = \$13.75$

Page 7
1. 35   2. 6.8   3. 9   4. 26   5. 16   6. 0
7. -16, -13, 6, 14   8. -33, -18, 0, 5
9. -36, -34, -32, -28, -4
10. -24, -14, -6, 6, 14

Page 8
1. >   2. >   3. >   4. <   5. >   6. >
7. $\frac{4}{5}, \frac{7}{8}, \frac{7}{5}$ 8. $\frac{3}{4}, \frac{2}{3}, \frac{1}{6}, \frac{1}{2}$
9. $\frac{8}{8}, \frac{5}{8}, \frac{1}{8}, \frac{5}{8}$ 10. $\frac{4}{9}, \frac{4}{8}, \frac{4}{5}, \frac{4}{2}$

Page 9
1. 16   2. -20   3. 13.86   4. -0.07
5. $\frac{1}{5}$ 6. -1   7. $\frac{1}{2}$ 8. $\frac{11}{24}$
9. 7   10. -283

Page 10
1. ⁻6   2. 0   3. 22   4. 7
5. 300   6. ⁻4.9   7. 13.3   8. ⁻1.53
9. $\frac{1}{8}$ 10. $\frac{1}{156}$

Page 11
1. 42   2. ⁻120   3. ⁻1,200   4. 182.7
5. $\frac{2}{45}$ 6. $⁻2\frac{1}{2}$ 7. 0   8. ⁻60
9. 360   10. ⁻0.207

Page 12
1. ⁻4   2. ⁻9   3. ⁻8   4. ⁻9   5. 0
6. undefined   7. $\frac{25}{48}$ 8. $\frac{9}{25}$ 9. $-1\frac{1}{8}$
10. $⁻2\frac{22}{25}$

Page 13
1. $7x - 49$ 2. $⁻5y + 20$ 3. $3x - 6y$
4. $⁻4x + 8y - 12$
5. $18x - 24y + 48z$
6. $⁻2.52x + 4.83y - 2.31$
7. $⁻24x - 16y + 48$
8. $12a - 15b + 21$
9. $4x - 6y$
10. $⁻\frac{5}{6}x + \frac{5}{12}y - 10$

Page 14
1. $4y$ 2. $⁻3x$ 3. $5a$
4. $0.5m$ 5. $6x + 3y$ 6. $3y + 3z$
7. $28a - 13b - 13c$ 8. $8p - 18$
9. $\frac{3}{5}y + \frac{1}{5}x$ 10. $18a - 2b$

Page 15
1. $3y - 10$ 2. ⁻5   3. $⁻2b + 8$
4. $6m + 5$ 5. $4y - 12$ 6. $8x - 5$
7. $13y - 12x$ 8. $16a - b$ 9. 0
10. $⁻x - 2y$

Page 16
1. $y = 9$ 2. $x = 11$ 3. $a = ⁻7$
4. $m = ⁻11$ 5. $x = 11$ 6. $y = 11$
7. $x = 21$ 8. $m = ⁻2$ 9. $y = ⁻8$
10. $y = 13$

Page 17
1. $m = 14$ 2. $x = 1$ 3. $x = 2$
4. $a = ⁻1\frac{2}{3}$ 5. $b = 10$ 6. $m = 10$
7. $y = 8\frac{2}{3}$ 8. $x = 5$ 9. $y = ⁻8$
10. $n = ⁻8$

© RBP Books   Algebra I Grades 5–8—RBP0105

Answer Pages

Page 18
1. $m = 7$ or $m = {}^-7$
2. $x = 5$ or $x = {}^-5$
3. $x = 18$ or $x = {}^-18$
4. $m = 7$ or $m = {}^-7$
5. $a = 7$ or $a = {}^-7$
6. $x = \frac{-1}{7}$ or $x = 1$
7. $x = 16$ or $x = 4$
8. $n = 7$ or $n = {}^-1$
9. $y = {}^-3$ or $y = 2\frac{1}{4}$
10. $x = {}^-1$ or $x = 2$

Page 19
1. $y = {}^-4$
2. $y = 3$
3. $x = 4$
4. $x = {}^-5$
5. $b = 3$
6. $m = 12$
7. $y = 3$
8. $p = {}^-10$
9. $m = {}^-1$
10. $x = 12$ or $x = {}^-12$
11. $y = {}^-1$ or $y = \frac{1}{5}$
12. $x = 2$ or $x = {}^-8$

Page 20
1. $r = \frac{d}{t}$
2. $t = \frac{d}{r}$
3. $p = \frac{I}{rt}$
4. $r = \frac{I}{pt}$
5. $\pi = \frac{A}{r^2}$
6. $r^2 = \frac{A}{\pi}$
7. $w = \frac{p - 2l}{2}$
8. $r = \frac{C}{2\pi}$
9. $b = \frac{2A}{h}$
10. $m = \frac{E}{c^2}$

Page 21
1. $x > 7$
2. $y \leq {}^-21$
3. $a < {}^-19$
4. $m \geq 0$
5. $x > {}^-1$
6. $b \leq 9.2$
7. $m < \frac{1}{9}$
8. $c \geq \frac{1}{2}$
9. $x < \frac{2}{9}$
10. $m < 21$

Page 22
1. $x \geq {}^-4$
2. $m > {}^-8$
3. $y \geq 5$
4. $p > {}^-20$
5. $x > \frac{1}{2}$
6. $y \leq \frac{1}{8}$
7. $x \leq {}^-0.7$
8. $n < {}^-3$

Page 23
1. $x \leq 5$
2. $x < {}^-6$
3. $y \leq {}^-3$
4. $x > {}^-5$
5. $m < {}^-2\frac{1}{2}$
6. $a \leq {}^-4\frac{1}{3}$
7. $x < 1\frac{4}{5}$
8. $b > 2$
9. $m < {}^-25$
10. $x \geq {}^-3$

Page 24
1. $y > 9$;
2. $x \leq 5$;
3. $y > {}^-7$;
4. $m \geq 7$;
5. $x > 6$;
6. $a < {}^-3$;
7. $c \geq {}^-6$;
8. $m \geq 3$;

Page 25
1. 3^9
2. 9^{15}
3. $({}^-5)^7$
4. x^{13}
5. y^{13}
6. m^3
7. $x^5 y^{10}$
8. $3^2 a^6 b^8$
9. $b^7 c^6 d^2$
10. $2^2 x^4 y^4$
11. $m^6 n^{10}$
12. $x^4 y^3 z^5$

Page 26
1. 6^4
2. 4^4
3. n
4. x^3
5. a^3
6. $m^4 n^3$
7. a
8. $4x^3$
9. $x^3 y^2$
10. $5a^2$

Page 27
1. $\frac{1}{4^3}$
2. $\frac{1}{5^4}$
3. $\frac{1}{m^6}$
4. $\frac{1}{(3y)^2}$
5. $\frac{7}{n^4}$
6. $\frac{c}{d^5}$
7. 256
8. m^{32}
9. $16t^4$
10. $27x^6$
11. $\frac{9}{a^4}$
12. $\frac{a^3 b^6}{c^3}$

Page 28
1. ^-12y
2. $^-x^2$
3. m^2
4. $8p^7$
5. $^-y^8$
6. $30n^6$
7. $a^5 b^5$
8. $^-27x^4 y^5$
9. $^-16m^6 n^6$
10. $^-48c^6$

Page 29
1. m^3
2. $\frac{3}{2}x$
3. b^5
4. $\frac{4}{c^3}$
5. $^-4x^5$
6. $^-4$
7. m^5
8. $^-8y^5$
9. $\frac{-5}{7}m^5 n^4$
10. $^-4a^5$

Page 30
1. $^-13y^3 + 2y - 32$
2. $7n^3 - n - 8$
3. $11y^2 - 4$
4. $5c^4$
5. $5x^3 + 3xy^2$
6. $^-15a^2 b^2 - 2ab$
7. $^-7xy^2 + 5xy$
8. $m^3 + m^2 n^2 - m^2 - 2$
9. $3x^2 y$

Page 31
1. $a^2 + 6a$
2. $32y^4 + 4y^2 + y$
3. $4m^5 + 13m^2 + 5m - 3$
4. $^-x^3 + 7x^2 + x - 10$
5. $10x^7 + 6x^5 - 10x^4 + 8x^2 + 2$
6. $5b^3 - 7a^2 b^2 + 4ab + 3$
7. $^-2y^3 - 3x^2 y^4 + 3x^2 - 2x + 6$
8. $^-2m^4 n^3 + 6m^3 n^3 - 2m^2 + 2mn^2 + 9$
9. $^-x^2 y + 8xy^2 - 3xy - 2$

Answer Pages

Page 32
1. $2a^4 + 6$
2. $^-5x^3 + 4x^2 + 3x + 12$
3. $8y^3 - 8y^2 - 5y + 16$
4. $9m^3 + 3m^2 + 2m - 1$
5. $6x^4 - 5x^3 + 5x - 4$
6. $^-5t^5 + 8t^4 - 3t^2 + 3t + 1$
7. $3y^3 - 2y^2 - 2y + 2$
8. $n^5 + 5n^4 + 2n^3 + 14n + 3$
9. $7ab^5 + b^4 + ab^4 - 4ab^3 + 3b^2 + 1$

Page 33
1. $30c^2 + 18c$
2. $^-12m^5 + 8m^2$
3. $15x^3 - 5x^2$
4. $^-6m^4 - m^2n$
5. $8y^3 + 10y^2 - 4y$
6. $12a^3 - 8a^2 + 20a$
7. $3x^9 - 6x^8 - 3x^6$
8. $^-2n^7 - 4n^6 + 2n^5 + 2n^4$
9. $^-3a^4b + 3a^2b^2 - 18a^3b$
10. $^-5xy^4 - 5x^2y^2 + 25x^2$

Page 34
1. $x^2 - 9$
2. $x^2 + x - 12$
3. $2x^2 + 10x + 8$
4. $8a^2 + 16a + 6$
5. $x^3 + x^2 + 2x + 2$
6. $9b^2 - 16$
7. $y^4 + 2y^3 - 3y - 6$
8. $5x^3 - 20x^2 + 4x - 16$
9. $4x^5 + 5x^4 + x^3$
10. $3x^9 + 11x^6 + 6x^3$

Page 35
1. $m^3 + 2m + 3$
2. $6a^3 - 7a^2 + 1$
3. $3x^4 - 4x^3 - 7x^2 + 12x - 6$
4. $n^6 - 2n^5 + n^3$
5. $x^4 - x^3 - x + 1$
6. $15m^5 - 5m^4 + 15m^3 - 25m^2 - 20$
7. $^-4y^4 + 4y^3 + 19y^2 - 4y - 15$
8. $x^4 - 1$

Page 36
1. $y(y + 5)$
2. $4x(x - 1)$
3. $17m^3(m + 3)$
4. $4(n^2 - n + 4)$
5. $3x^2y(2 + y)$
6. $n(5m^4n^3 - 3m^3 + 30n^2)$
7. $a(a^8 + a^6 - a^3 - a + 1)$
8. $xy^2(5x^2 - 15y + 20x - 1)$

Page 37
1. $(x - 5)^2$
2. $(x + 8)^2$
3. $(x + 3)^2$
4. $(x + 7)^2$
5. $(x - 1)^2$
6. $(a + 3b)^2$
7. $(4x - 5y)^2$
8. $(3x - 5)^2$
9. $(2x^2 + 4)^2$
10. $(3x^2 - y)^2$

Page 38
1. $(x - 3)(x - 5)$
2. $(x + 6)(x + 4)$
3. $(x - 9)(x + 5)$
4. $(x + 7)(x + 4)$
5. $(x - 9)(x - 5)$
6. $(x + 7)(x + 3)$
7. $(x - 25)(x + 4)$
8. $2(x + 2)^2$
9. $(3x - 4)(x + 1)$
10. $(2x + 5)(2x - 3)$

Page 39
1. $x = 7$ or $x = -4$
2. $x = ^-4$ or $x = 3$
3. $x = ^-9$ or $x = 3$
4. $x = ^-2$ or $x = ^-3$
5. $x = 7$ or $x = 2$
6. $x = ^-8$ or $x = \frac{9}{2}$
7. $x = ^-3$ or $x = 3$
8. $w = ^-1$ or $w = \frac{2}{3}$
9. $x = 0$ or $x = \frac{2}{3}$
10. $x = ^-1$ or $x = \frac{5}{3}$

Page 40
1. $\frac{x + 4}{8x}$
2. $\frac{y - 2}{y}$
3. $\frac{m - 4}{m}$
4. x
5. $\frac{1}{x - 8}$
6. $x - 1$
7. $\frac{5}{x + 6}$
8. $^-3$
9. $\frac{x + 1}{2x + 1}$
10. $^-2$

Page 41
1. $\frac{3}{2}$
2. $\frac{4}{3ab}$
3. $2x^2$
4. $\frac{^-3c^4}{c + 3}$
5. $\frac{x + 3}{(x^2 - 2)(x - 3)}$
6. $\frac{x + 4}{x - 4}$
7. $\frac{4}{(x + 2)(x - 1)}$
8. $\frac{x}{x + 2}$

Page 42
1. $\frac{5x}{16}$
2. $\frac{1}{3x}$
3. $\frac{3x^2}{7}$
4. $\frac{2}{3}$
5. $\frac{8}{3}$
6. $\frac{(x + 1)^2}{x}$
7. 1
8. $\frac{(x + 6)(x + 4)}{(x + 3)(x - 2)}$

Page 43
1. $\frac{2m}{y}$
2. $\frac{^-4x - 12}{x - 6}$
3. $\frac{^-x + 2}{x + 1}$
4. 4
5. $\frac{2a^2 - 6a + 4}{2a - 1}$
6. $\frac{3x^2 - 10x - 8}{x + 4}$
7. $\frac{^-2x^2 - 7x}{2x + 1}$
8. $\frac{x^2 + 4x + 1}{5x + 1}$

Page 44
1. $c = ^-3$ or $c = ^-1$
2. $x = \frac{30}{11}$
3. $b = ^-2$
4. $y = 3$
5. $a = \frac{^-13}{2}$
6. $x = \frac{17}{2}$
7. $x = \frac{4}{21}$
8. $a = \frac{5}{3}$

Answer Pages

Page 45

1. $4|x|$ **2.** $|x - 4|$

3. x^5 **4.** x^7

5. $x^7 \sqrt{x}$ **6.** $5(x + 5)^3$

7. $2x^3 \sqrt{3x}$ **8.** $15x^2y \sqrt{y}$

9. $6x^2y^4 \sqrt{x}$ **10.** $(x + 2)^5$

Page 46

1. $5\sqrt{3}$ **2.** $6\sqrt{3x}$

3. $6\sqrt{xy}$ **4.** $7\sqrt{5xy}$

5. $\sqrt{20x + 10}$ **6.** $2x^3y^3 \sqrt{3}$

7. $5xy \sqrt{2xy}$ **8.** $a\sqrt{bc}$

9. $x^{107}y^{14} \sqrt{xy}$ **10.** $(x + 5)^7 \sqrt{x + 5}$

Page 47

1. $\frac{4}{5}$ **2.** $\frac{1}{2}$

3. $\sqrt{6}$ **4.** $x^3 \sqrt{3}$

5. $3x$ **6.** $\sqrt{2}$

7. $\frac{2 \sqrt{x}}{x}$ **8.** $\frac{6x \sqrt{5}}{5}$

Page 48

1. $7\sqrt{5}$ **2.** $4\sqrt{2}$

3. $12\sqrt{x}$ **4.** $14\sqrt{2}$

5. $5\sqrt{5}$ **6.** $\sqrt{5}$

7. $(3x^2 + 2)\sqrt{x}$ **8.** $3\sqrt{2x + 2}$

9. $(x^3 + 2)\sqrt{x^3 - 1}$ **10.** $\frac{2}{3}\sqrt{3}$ or $\frac{2\sqrt{3}}{3}$

Page 49

1. $x = 121$ **2.** $x = 27.04$ **3.** $x = \frac{64}{3}$

4. $x = 396$ **5.** $x = 84$ **6.** $x = 5$

7. $x = 3$ **8.** $x = 5$

Page 50

1. $x = 0$ or $x = {}^-7$ **2.** $x = 0$ or $x = {}^-2$

3. $x = 0$ or $x = \frac{3}{7}$ **4.** $x = 0$ or $x = {}^-1$

5. $x = {}^-6$ or $x = {}^-1$ **6.** $x = 8$ or $x = {}^-6$

7. $x = {}^-3$ **8.** $x = {}^-5$ or $x = {}^-1$

Page 51

1. $x = 1$ or $x = {}^-15$

2. $x = \frac{7}{2} + \sqrt{14.25}$ or $x = \frac{7}{2} - \sqrt{14.25}$

3. $x = {}^-3$ or $x = {}^-5$

4. $x = 1 + \sqrt{11}$ or $x = 1 - \sqrt{11}$

5. $x = {}^-1 + \sqrt{6}$ or $x = {}^-1 - \sqrt{6}$

6. $x = 5$ or $x = {}^-\frac{1}{2}$ **7.** $x = \frac{5}{3}$ or $x = {}^-1$

8. $x = \frac{2}{3}$ or $x = {}^-\frac{5}{2}$

Page 52

1. $x = 5 \pm \sqrt{3}$ **2.** $x = \frac{-4}{3}$ or $x = 2$

3. no real solutions   **4.** $x = \dfrac{5 \pm \sqrt{33}}{4}$

Page 53

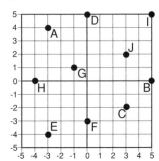

Page 54

1. 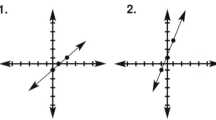   **2.**

3. 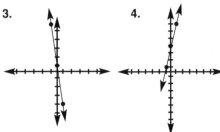   **4.**

5. 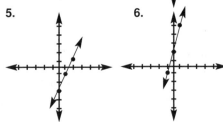   **6.**

Answer Pages

Page 55

1.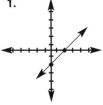

2.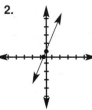

3.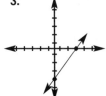

4.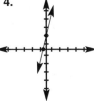

5.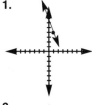

6.

Page 56

1. 7   **2.** $\frac{1}{4}$ **3.** $\frac{-2}{3}$ **4.** $\frac{-1}{2}$

5. ‾2   **6.** $\frac{-11}{8}$ **7.** 4   **8.** $\frac{12}{5}$

Page 57

1.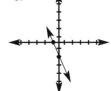

2.

3.

4.

5.

6.

Page 58

1. $y = ‾2x - 6$ **2.** $y = 6x - 13$ **3.** $y = ‾3x + 3$

4. $y = 3x + 7$ **5.** $y = \frac{1}{2}x + 3$ **6.** $y = \frac{1}{2}x + 2$

Page 59

1. $y = \frac{2}{7}x + \frac{17}{7}$ **2.** $y = \frac{-3}{2}x + \frac{13}{2}$ **3.** $y = \frac{1}{2}x$

4. $y = \frac{1}{2}x - 2$ **5.** $y = \frac{-2}{3}x + \frac{14}{3}$ **6.** $y = \frac{3}{2}x + 6$

Page 60

1. (0,5)

2. (‾3,‾3)

3. (‾8,‾7)

4.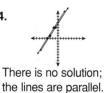

There is no solution; the lines are parallel.

Page 61

1. (1,6)   **2.** $(\frac{-15}{2},25)$ **3.** (2,‾4)   **4.** (6,3)

5. (4,‾2)   **6.** Infinitely many solutions

Page 62

1. (5,‾2)   **2.** (3,5)   **3.** $(2,\frac{4}{5})$

4. $(\frac{1}{2},3)$ **5.** (1,4)   **6.** (2,5)

Page 63

1.

2.

3.

4.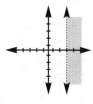

5.

6.

    Algebra I Grades 5–8—RBP0105

Answer Pages

Page 64

1.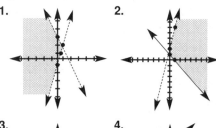

2.

3.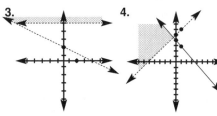

4.

5.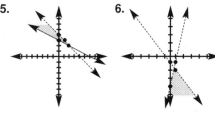

6.

Page 65

1. x + 2,300 = 29,100; x = $26,800

2. $\frac{50}{7}$ • 2 = x; x = about 16 quarters
(8 quarters for each load)

3. x + 2x = 36; x = $12.00

4. 50x = 1,850; x = 37 paintings

5. 4.99 + 0.30(36) = c; c = $15.79

Page 66

1. $\frac{13}{310} = \frac{x}{475}$; x = about 20 gallons

2. $\frac{2}{8} = \frac{x}{120}$; x = 30 adults

3. $\frac{7}{25} = \frac{x}{425}$; x = 119 students

4. $\frac{1}{4.2} = \frac{12.5}{x}$; x = 52.5 km

5. $\frac{3}{5} = \frac{x}{220}$; 132 + 220 = 352 students

6. $\frac{18}{1} = \frac{x}{7}$; x = 126 minutes or

2 hours, 6 minutes

Page 67

1. $100 million

2. the $19,000/year job

3. 12,775 employees

4. $19,026.90

Page 68

1. A   **2.** C   **3.** B   **4.** D
5. B   **6.** D   **7.** A

Page 69

1. 48   **2.** 98   **3.** 96 sheets
4. 205 cm   **5.** $21.45

Page 70

1. c   **2.** 12 minutes

3. Ronnie: $7,500; Kenny: $7,000

4. Bob, Sam, Ricky, Craig, Taylor

5. Rachel—tennis; Charla—volleyball;
Robert—racquetball;
Kenneth—basketball

Page 71

1. 300 sq. feet **2.** 440 miles **3.** $850
4. 2 hours   **5.** 330 mph

Page 72

1. 88%   **2.** 27%
3. $36.54; $558.49
4. total cost: $25.67
5. 20%